Incredible
AUSTRALIA

Near Warragul, Victoria

Incredible
AUSTRALIA

JOCELYN BURT

DENT

Melbourne

Acknowledgements

I would like to thank Dick Lang of Desert-Trek Australia, Adelaide, for the trips into the Simpson and Sturt's Stony deserts; Doug Fearon of Austrek Safaris, Cairns, for the trip to Escott Station, Gulf of Carpentaria; Quicksilver Connections Ltd, Port Douglas, for the trips to the Great Barrier Reef; the National Parks & Wildlife Service in New South Wales; Ron and Valerie Taylor/ANT Photo Library for the underwater view of coral reproduced on page 71; Klaus Uhlenhut/ANT Photo Library for the frilled lizard reproduced on page 77; and the Victorian Tourism Commission for the penguins reproduced on page 75.

First published in 1988 by
J. M. Dent Pty Limited
112 Lewis Rd, Knoxfield 3180, Victoria, Australia
© Jocelyn Burt 1988

National Library of Australia
Cataloguing-in-Publication entry:

Burt, Jocelyn.
   Incredible Australia.

   ISBN 0 86770 080 7.

   1. Australia—Description and travel—
   1976-   —Views. I. Title.

994.06'3'0222

Designed by Noni Edmunds
Typeset in Vladimir by Solo Typesetting, South Australia
Printed in Hong Kong by South China Printing Co.

Contents

Gosford, New South Wales

About Australia

Australia is not only the world's largest island and smallest continent but also its flattest landmass: more than half of the country is less than 300 metres above sea-level, and only five percent rises above 600 metres. It is old too. Some of its land-surfaces have been exposed above the sea for a much longer period than those in other parts of the world; and the geological forces that during an earlier age formed much of the earth into high mountain-ranges did not affect Australia. As a result, the continent's surface has had time to settle down and has been worn and sculpted only by the elements. The land looks old, especially when it is seen from the air during a drought, with every ridge and gully, dune and plain laid bare.

Many people overseas imagine the whole of the Australian continent to be dry, dusty and eternally hot, a land where the sun shines every day, the coastline is one ongoing sweep of wide sandy beaches, the only vegetation to be seen is gumtrees, and the only animals to be sighted are kangaroos, koalas, strange lizards and sheep. Often they are astonished to learn that although a large portion of the country is hot, dry and dusty, there are areas dominated by all shades of green, rather than browns, reds and yellows; that there is a multitude of lakes and billabongs surrounded by lush vegetation; that verdant valleys fed by wide rivers lie at the feet of mountains densely covered with forests of trees other than eucalypts, watered by up to 5000 millimetres of rain annually; and that for a few months of the year the area of mountain country covered in snow is greater than the whole of Switzerland!

Fortunately, an unprecedented number of people from all over the world are now coming to Australia and finding that there is a lot more to this land than their preconceived ideas allowed. Although Australians have long been aware that their country *is* a special place, with an unusual character and wonderful scenery, it has not been until recent times that so many thousands from all walks of life have made the most of weekends, holidays, long-service leaves and retirements to explore their country. Locals and overseas visitors alike are discovering its unique beauty, and its stunning contrasts: between forested mountains and harsh deserts, tropical regions and cool temperate zones, the great natural wonders and those made by man in the modern cities. They are fascinated by the hosts of unusual birds and animals, by the abundance of interesting trees and plants, and by the mineral riches. Even the 38 000 kilometres of coastline—aside from the superb wide sandy beaches for which Australia is famous—contain an enormous diversity of scenic beauty, colour and character.

Australia is a big country, with three different timezones. Many motorists discover its great size only when they start to travel around it. The land-area is roughly equal to that of the United States (excluding Alaska). The mainland stretches about 3200 kilometres from the most northerly point of Cape York to Wilsons Promontory in the south; and the distance from west to east—Steep Point, between Carnarvon and Kalbarri, to Cape Byron at Byron Bay—measures about 4000 kilometres. An extensive network of aerial services extends over the continent, and every year motoring is being made easier by the upgrading of roads: it is now possible to drive around Australia and stay on the bitumen. Although conventional cars can get to many places 'off the beaten track', there are still plenty of spots worth visiting that are accessible only by four-wheel-drive vehicles. For people without such vehicles, there is a wide choice of commercial safari outfits willing to take them there.

To appreciate fully the beauty and the ever-changing moods of the Australian countryside, it is often necessary to spend some time in the places visited. It is not enough to rush through without stopping, or to venture only a few metres from a parked vehicle. Sometimes visitors not familiar with a place will not respond to it immediately, especially if they arrive at their destination travel-weary, or in the middle of the day when the sun is high and hot. Many of the places come into the fullness of their beauty early or late in the day, when the sun is low in the sky and colours become more vibrant. Even already impressive landscapes are then transformed into sights of exquisite loveliness and grandeur.

Where, people may ask, is the soul of Australia? Many believe that it lies somewhere in the worn land of the continent's centre, where the stark and strangely beautiful landscapes reflect the Dreaming of the Aborigines and the genesis of time. For others it may lie deep in a forested mountain gorge, or along a slowly moving river lined with magnificent stands of river red gums, or on a long sandy beach washed by rolling waves capped with plumes of flying white spray. Where exactly the spirit resides does not matter. Everyone will find it in a different place.

Do try to discover it for yourself, because as you explore this incredible country, you will indeed be rewarded.

Sunrise from Powers lookout, near Whitfield, Victoria

The Cities

Australia is an urban society and the settlement of its 16 million inhabitants, representing some 150 different cultures, is concentrated in the coastal regions, especially the moister eastern and south-eastern seaboard. Of the eight State capitals — Canberra, Sydney, Melbourne, Brisbane, Adelaide, Perth, Hobart and Darwin — only Canberra, the nation's capital, lies inland; even the two largest provincial cities, Newcastle in New South Wales and Geelong in Victoria, are on the coast. And of the more than 10 million who live in all these cities, two-thirds populate Sydney and Melbourne.

Australia's cities are comparatively young, and it is only since the Second World War that most of the State capitals have shed their 'town' images and gained distinctive urban atmospheres. Today the hearts of most of the cities are marked by clusters of modern highrise edifices towering over the older buildings and fashionable malls. Sprawling beyond the inner-city areas are the suburbs, moving further out each year as new estates cater for the great Australian dream of a fenced-off plot of land with a house and garden.

Many of the provincial cities are also steadily expanding, and developing individual characters. Newcastle has a population twice that of Hobart; Geelong's matches that of the Tasmanian capital. Some of Queensland's cities are mushrooming in development, and places like Cairns and Townsville now have their own highrise buildings; the Gold Coast, containing some of Australia's richest real estate, has had them for years. In central Australia, Alice Springs has in a very short time evolved from a rough and dusty village to a shiny modern township.

Australia is a large country, and its major cities are separated by considerable distances. Sydney and Canberra are the two that lie closest to each other, with a road distance of 300 kilometres between them. From Sydney, Melbourne lies 880 kilometres to the south, and Brisbane 1020 kilometres to the north; further still is Cairns, 1720 kilometres north from Brisbane. Hobart, on the south-eastern coast of the island State of Tasmania (separated from the mainland by Bass Strait), is 650 kilometres from Melbourne; while from that city, Adelaide to the west is 730 kilometres away. The two most isolated cities are Perth in Western Australia and Darwin in the Northern Territory: from Adelaide, Perth is 2700 kilometres to the west, and Darwin, a city even more remotely placed on the far north coast, is 3020 kilometres away.

Canberra, in the Australian Capital Territory, is the
federal capital. The only Australian capital city to emerge
during the twentieth century, it was established in 1911
and built to a specified plan. Although the States federated
in 1901, it was eight years before an acceptable site was
chosen. Canberra has grown into a beautiful industry-
free garden city noted for its impressive buildings, among
them the Australian War Memorial, the High Court, the
marble-columned National Library, and the new Parliament House, set on Capital Hill. This view (*above*) is
from Mount Ainslie; it shows the War Memorial and
Anzac Parade, with both the old and the new Parliament
House in the distance.

Adelaide, in South Australia, is the State's capital and
was founded in 1836. The city lies on a long, narrow
plain beside Gulf St Vincent, bordered on its eastern
side by the picturesque Adelaide Hills. It is the best-
planned of all the State capitals, and the easiest for
motorists to negotiate. Every two years in March the city
stages the Adelaide Festival of Arts, Australia's most
important cultural festival. A major venue for theatrical
and musical performances during this event is the Festival
Centre (*left*) set in the gardens by Torrens Lake.

9

Sydney, the capital of New South Wales, is the first city and seaport of Australia. It was settled in January 1788 when a party of British soldiers and convicts landed at Sydney Cove to establish a penal colony and inaugurate the European settlement of Australia. Today it is the busiest port in the South Pacific, and boasts one of the world's most magnificent harbours, made even more splendid by landmarks such as the Sydney Opera House and the Harbour Bridge (*above*). Sydney is also renowned for its surf beaches; the one at Manly (*right*) is among the best-known in Australia. In the busy city centre, Martin Place (*left*) has long been a popular meeting-point with Sydneysiders.

11

Hobart is the capital of the island State of Tasmania. Although it has the smallest population of all the capitals, it is the second-oldest, having been settled in 1803. Two-thirds of its first residents were convicts, and for many years it was a boisterous whaling port; today it is the quietest of all the capitals. The setting is superb, for the city nestles in the rolling hills by the beautiful Derwent River estuary, guarded by majestic Mount Wellington. Hobart and the entire island are rich in history; some of the most interesting old buildings in the city lie around Constitution and Victoria docks (*above*).

Melbourne, capital of Victoria, is Australia's second-largest city after Sydney, and is situated by the banks of the Yarra River (*top left*). Settled in 1835, it was one of the few major cities to be founded as a free settlement rather than as a penal colony; two decades later the Victorian goldrush quickly transformed the small village into a dignified city. Melbourne still retains its graciousness, with its lovely central parks and gardens, and its wide treelined streets such as Collins Street (*left*). It is the only Australian city to have a large network of trams, and the only one to have hosted the Olympic Games.

Darwin, in the Northern Territory, lies on the isolated north coast of Australia, in a region known popularly as the 'Top End'. This tropical city, the capital of the Territory, has the highest growth-rate in the country; it is also the gateway to Asia, and to the north's exciting hinterland. Darwin was established in 1869; earlier, there were several unsuccessful attempts to settle the area, the first being in 1842, but the hostile environment and extreme isolation proved too much for the struggling pioneers. The city was rebuilt after Cyclone Tracy devastated it in 1974. This was not a new experience: reconstruction had taken place after two earlier cyclones, as well as after the bombing by the Japanese in 1942. The Smith Street Mall (*above*) is located in the heart of the city.

Gold Coast, Queensland. Spreading along the surf beach on its eastern seaboard and the winding Nerang River to the west, Surfers Paradise (*above*) is the most renowned of all the communities that comprise the City of Gold Coast. The city stretches for about 32 kilometres along the subtropical coast from just south of Brisbane to the New South Wales border, and has become Australia's most glamorous aquatic playground. It was constituted a city in 1959, and since then millions of dollars have been spent—and continue to be spent—in establishing hotels, highrise holiday and residential apartments, luxury homes on canal waterways, and amusement centres of every description. Immediately behind the Gold Coast lies the beautiful McPherson Range, where day trippers can explore the many natural attractions.

Brisbane, the capital of Queensland, is built around the busiest commercial river in Australia, the Brisbane River (*left*). The city was founded in 1823, and over the years it has grown into the country's third-largest metropolis. One of the city centre's attractions is the Queen Street Mall (*right*). Another outstanding feature is the Queensland Cultural Centre, which incorporates the performing-arts complex, the State Museum, the Queensland Art Gallery and the State Library; all are situated on the landscaped bank of the Brisbane River and are within walking distance of the city centre. Brisbane staged the World Expo '88, as part of Australia's Bicentenary celebrations.

Perth is the capital of Western Australia. Founded in 1829, it has developed into a beautiful city that spreads around the banks of the Swan River. One of its greatest assets is Kings Park (*above*), the 400 hectares of native bushland overlooking the inner city. Situated only 19 kilometres south of Perth is the State's chief port, Fremantle, a city renowned for its historic buildings and magnificent marina and yachting complex. During the summer of 1986–87 Fremantle played host to the crews of the America's Cup challengers, and, together with Perth, to the thousands of visitors who flocked to the West for the event.

The Coastline

Some of Australia's grandest scenery is to be found around the diverse and colourful coastline. Forested mountains and coastal plains end abruptly at boulder-strewn shores or sheer off into spectacular, sometimes terrifyingly steep cliffs; remarkable landforms occur in many places, some boldly prominent, others concealing their unusual formations in wild and rugged terrain; inlets and lagoons offer tranquillity; and estuaries, sandbarred or widely flowing, gently punctuate the seaboard in many places—spots where it is not hard to find peace and contentment, especially in the early and late hours of the day.

Australia's magnificent wide beaches are the most popular of all the coastal features, and have long been famous throughout the world. They sweep around the coastline, giving way in places to rocky headlands and cliffs, or to mudflats laced with dense colonies of mangroves. Some run virtually unbroken for distances of well over 100 kilometres; others are pocket-sized and secluded, tucked away between areas of rock. The sands of these beaches vary in colour from pure white through all shades of yellow and light-brown to red.

The colours of the sea vary enormously too, depending on climate and location. The deep greens and blues of southern coastal waters change to vibrant turquoise and aquamarine in the warm north. In some places, particularly around the south-west coast of Western Australia, the colours often appear in striations that vary from the palest of greens near the shore to a dark inky blue further out.

Scores of islands lie offshore, many of them very beautiful, with more than a hint of romance. They range from small outcrops of rock, shallow mudflats or low-lying coral islets, through palm-fringed hilly islands, to vast mountainous masses; some of the loveliest lie off the north-eastern coast of Queensland and have become popular holiday playgrounds for thousands of Australians and overseas visitors. It is in this region that the greatest coastal feature of all is situated: the Great Barrier Reef. One of the natural wonders of the world, this beautiful complex of coral reefs, lagoons, channels, continental islands and coral cays provides Australia with a priceless natural heritage.

Australians love their coastline, and enjoy the many attractions it has to offer. Its many contrasting faces and ever-changing moods evoke different responses in different people; but once caught in the spell of that marvellous combination of sea and shore, the visitor is drawn back time and time again.

Laurieton (NSW) lies a short distance off the Pacific Highway, about 215 kilometres north of Newcastle. From the spectacular North Brother Mountain lookout (*above*) there are aerial-like views over the coast, the Camden Haven River estuary, Indian Head at the northern end of Crowdy National Park, and the lovely Queens and Watson Taylor lakes. The lookout is only four kilometres out of Laurieton, and access is via a steep but good bitumen road. From the carpark there are some lovely walking-tracks, which are maintained by the Forestry Commission of New South Wales.

Lakes Entrance (Vic.) is situated at the eastern end of the Gippsland Lakes, 313 kilometres from Melbourne, and has long been an important fishing base and popular holiday resort (*left*). The lakes comprise a large system of coastal lagoons that cover an area of nearly 400 square kilometres near Sale, in east Gippsland. Until a century ago they were virtually landlocked by the dunes of the Ninety Mile Beach, but in 1889 a channel was cut through the great sandbar at Lakes Entrance to enable steamers to enter the lakes from the sea. Today this channel is used by the fishing fleet.

Great Keppel Island (Qld) is one of the larger islands of the Great Barrier Reef, and lies off Rockhampton. On its western side there is a holiday resort. The island's outstanding feature is its beaches (*above*), which are among the finest to be found on the settled islands along the Queensland coast: long white stretches of sand sweeping from one rocky headland to another, some straight and wide enough to accommodate a landing aircraft.

Near Cairns (Qld). Some superb coastal scenery lies between Cairns and Port Douglas, and much of it can be seen from the Cook Highway, which links the two places. It is best not to be in a hurry when travelling this road: traffic is often heavy and there are few opportunities for overtaking on the long stretches that wind around the hillsides. Although many of the beaches along this section of coast are of fine sand, there are quite a few littered with stones of all shapes and sizes. This beach (*top right*) is just north of Ellis Beach, a popular spot with holidaymakers.

Surf carnival, Peterborough (Vic.). Surf lifesaving clubs from all over the State meet to compete in a number of events (*right*). This volunteer organization originated in Australia in the early 1900s, and today there are around 65 000 lifesavers patrolling Australian surfing beaches.

Torndirrup National Park (WA) lies 20 kilometres south of Albany, and covers part of the promontory bordering King George Sound. With its wild granite slopes pushing boldly into the turbulent Southern Ocean, and its variety of coastal landforms, the scenery in this region is both unusual and thrilling. Fishing from the rocks can be very dangerous because of the unexpected king waves that periodically wash the shore. Shown here (*left*) is Salmon Holes Beach, a good place for walking and salmon-fishing; a few kilometres away is the old Albany whaling station, now a museum.

Broome (WA), in the Kimberley region of the continent's far north-west, 2213 kilometres from Perth, has some of the most colourful coastal scenery in Australia. This view (*above*) is at Roebuck Bay, near the jetty, where a collection of red sandstone rocks, fashioned by the elements into fantastic shapes, stands in dramatic contrast to the turquoise-blue sea; the rest of the bay is lined with red sand and colonies of mangroves. Roebuck Bay is too dangerous for swimming because of the sharks, but there is safe water on the ocean side of the town at Cable Beach, where the water temperature is a delicious 26°C.

23

Port Campbell National Park (Vic.) covers 32 kilometres of coastline between Cape Otway and Warrnambool, in the west of the State. The Twelve Apostles (*top left*), shaped over the centuries by waves and weather, are just one of many grand sights along this coast. The most scenic access-route is via the Great Ocean Road, which runs between Geelong and Warrnambool.

Tasman Peninsula (Tas.) is linked by a thread of land only 71 metres wide to the Forestier Peninsula at Eaglehawk Neck. Lying on the east coast, 80 kilometres from Hobart, the Tasman Peninsula is renowned for its spectacular coastline and unusual landforms. This view (*left*) is of Pirates Bay, from the cliffs at Eaglehawk Neck.

Whitsunday Passage (Qld) has been acclaimed as one of the world's most beautiful waterways, and is a firm favourite with yachtsmen. Lying off Proserpine, it extends for over 30 kilometres along the coast, with a width in some places of less than three kilometres, and contains some of the loveliest islands of the Great Barrier Reef area. Many of these have holiday resorts, from where networks of delightful walking-tracks wind up to peaks and ridges that give glorious panoramas over the passage. Pictured (*above*) is the view from Spion Kop, on South Molle Island.

25

Fowlers Bay (SA) lies about 40 kilometres off the Eyre Highway, halfway between Ceduna and the head of the Great Australian Bight. The bay is bordered by massive dunes (*above*), sculpted by the wind and constantly on the move: in places they resemble scenes from the Sahara Desert. Visited by whalers during the first half of the nineteenth century, Fowlers Bay in the 1890s became a port for the shipping of primary produce. In 1840 the explorer Edward John Eyre used the place as a depot for stores for his epic journey along the coast to the west. Gradually the settlement became a ghost town, but in the 1980s people started to inhabit it again.

The Great Australian Bight is the vast curve that sweeps against the underbelly of the continent in two States, South Australia and Western Australia. Much of this windswept area is edged by the world's longest line of unbroken cliffs (*right*), in places stretching for around 200 kilometres and plunging to depths of up to 150 metres. At the various viewing-areas that lie close to the Eyre Highway in South Australia, notices warn of the dangerous cliff overhangs, which look alarmingly fragile when seen from further along the edge; indeed, it is easy to stand on one of these without knowing it. Take care if there is a strong north wind blowing!

Mountains and Ranges

Seen from the air, most of Australia's weatherworn, comparatively low mountains and ranges appear as a series of gentle folds, rather crumpled and creased in aspect. There is no hint of the wonderful beauty they contain, or of the true nature of much of the terrain, which in many places is wild and rugged, marked with sheer escarpments, deep gorges, densely forested slopes and bold jagged cliffs.

In a country as flat as Australia, any mountain is of consequence: the fact that it may be a mere hill compared with the mountains of the world does not bother Australians. The country has only one continental mountain chain, the eastern highlands, known as the Great Dividing Range. This comprises a series of ranges, plateaux, spurs and rolling hills that extend from Cape York in the far north to Victoria and Tasmania in the south. Like a mighty barrier, the Great Divide separates the fertile east coast from the vast tracts of arid inland plains. Some of its peaks easily reach 1600 metres: Queensland's highest, at 1611 metres, is Mount Bartle Frere, while Victoria's Mount Bogong rises to 1986 metres. But the highest country of all is in the Snowy Mountains, part of the Australian Alps, where boulder-studded Mount Kosciusko lords it over the ranges at 2228 metres. In winter the higher regions of southern New South Wales, Victoria and Tasmania are well covered in snow; in these areas a number of ski-resorts have been developed.

Of all Australia's mountains, those in Tasmania most resemble classical alpine scenery. With their serrated ridges and jagged peaks rearing above rugged plateaux, these ranges form part of an extensive wilderness area.

Other ranges in Australia differ vastly from the green slopes of the Great Dividing Range. Numerous hills, mesas and buttes sprawl over the north-western and central region. Rising abruptly from the plains, their extraordinarily colourful but dry, stony slopes support little plantlife other than spinifex; often they are topped with great collars of rock. Among well-known inland ranges are the MacDonnells, lying east and west of Alice Springs, and the Pilbara's formidable ironstone Hamersley Range, where the highest peak in Western Australia, Mount Bruce, reaches 1235 metres. South Australia's main mountain system is that of the Mount Lofty and Flinders ranges. The Mount Lofty Ranges start at the picturesque Adelaide Hills and eventually give way to the rugged Flinders Ranges.

Maleny (Qld) is situated in the beautiful hill country of the Great Dividing Range, 18 kilometres from Landsborough, just north of Brisbane. From Howells Knob lookout, five kilometres out of the Maleny township, there are wonderful panoramas of the surrounding rural land and of the distant Glasshouse Mountains (*above*) — the plugs of ancient volcanoes that once dominated this corner of south-east Queensland. These striking geological formations standing against the horizon reminded Captain Cook, in 1770, of the glass furnaces of industrial Yorkshire.

Near Yarram (Vic.) in the Strzelecki Ranges. South Gippsland is dominated by these beautiful ranges, where steep slopes, high ridges and forested gullies give way to gently rolling farmland. For quite a few kilometres the road from Yarram to Morwell follows the Tarra River, a small stream that runs through some lovely mountain-ash forests; the scene pictured (*left*) is south of Tarra Valley National Park. Although large tracts of mountain-ash have been cut down over the years, the Forests Commission has started an extensive reforestation programme in many parts of the ranges.

29

The MacDonnell Ranges (NT), rocky and colourful, extend approximately 65 kilometres eastward and 320 kilometres westward from Alice Springs in central Australia. Lying in its craggy folds are many spectacular gorges, gaps and chasms that attract thousands of visitors annually. The view shown here (*top left*) is near Glen Helen, 130 kilometres west of Alice Springs.

The Stirling Range (WA) rises abruptly over the vast agricultural plains about 80 kilometres north of Albany, in the south-west of the State. The range is an important national park, renowned for its profusion of wildflowers and its challenging walking-trails. Pictured (*left*) is the view from the eastern end of the Cranbrook road.

Kangaroo Valley (NSW) lies east of Moss Vale in the Southern Highlands, part of the Great Dividing Range. Early-morning mists, with the promise of a fine day, frequently blanket the valleys in this area. This view (*above*) is from Manning lookout, in Morton National Park, situated south of the Illawarra Highway. The Southern Highlands cover more than 2500 square kilometres of high plateau country dissected by dramatic gorges and escarpments; the best-known escarpment is the Illawarra, part of which runs through Morton National Park.

The Flinders Ranges (SA) begin just north of Adelaide and extend for nearly 400 kilometres. As they push north towards the desert plains and salty Lake Frome their slopes, peaks and gorges become wilder and more rugged. The best place to experience the magnificent scenery of the northern Flinders is at Arkaroola; from the tourist village runs the famous Ridge Tops Track, an extremely steep and rough track that winds tortuously along the tops of the razor-like ridges of the ranges. The scene shown (*above*) is of the Freeling Heights, from the Ridge Tops Track.

The Bungle Bungle Range (WA) is situated about 200 kilometres south of Kununurra, in the Kimberley region of the far north-west of the continent. Until 1983 only the local Aborigines and a few pastoralists knew of this astonishing range that rises from the plains in a mass of eroded, beehive-like domes (*right*) marked with steep narrow gorges and sheer cliffs. Today it is a national park, and many tourists see it either by air (from Kununurra or Halls Creek), or by taking the extremely rough four-wheel-drive track that runs from Turkey Creek to the edge of the range.

Baw Baw Plateau (Vic.) is in Gippsland, 180 kilometres from Melbourne. Rising to around 1400 metres, the granite plateau is in the southernmost part of Victoria's high country and consists of about eight square kilometres of undulating timbered ridges and open snow-plains. Most of the plateau is a national park, which provides some good bushwalking in summer and ski touring in winter. An area set aside for downhill skiing and a small ski-resort lie at the edge of the park, half an hour's drive from the little alpine village of Tanjilbren. In winter the snow gums are often laden with ice (*above*), and periodically the plateau's silence is broken by the sound of ice tumbling to the ground as an overweighted branch snaps under its burden.

The Western Arthur Range (Tas.) lies in the South West National Park, some 170 kilometres from Hobart. Access to much of this national park's beauty is difficult because it is a wilderness of high buttongrass plains, dense vegetation, glacial lakes and rugged mountains marked with jagged peaks and cliff-like faces; and the climate can be as formidable as the topography. The only way to see this park properly is to hike for many days; however, the manmade Lake Pedder edges the park, and there are some excellent views (*top right*) from the roads around the lake.

Mount Kosciusko (NSW), 2228 metres high, is Australia's highest mountain and lies in Kosciusko National Park, in the Australian Alps. In many places its slopes are strewn with fantastic granite boulders (*right*), which in winter are heavily blanketed with snow. During the summer months the walk to the summit from Thredbo is one of the most popular in the park.

Mount Buffalo (Vic.) lies in north-eastern Victoria and borders part of the Ovens Valley, which extends from Wangaratta to the rising slopes of Mount Feathertop. One of the oldest national parks in Australia, Mount Buffalo rises abruptly from the valley floor, its massive granite walls topped by a spacious plateau marked with outcrops of granite. Near the chalet, several lookouts perched in the granite at the plateau's edge give breath-taking views over the Ovens Valley and surrounding mountains (*above*). Hang-glider enthusiasts come from everywhere to make flights; indeed, the mountain has been declared one of the best venues in the world for this sport. A good bitumen road of 27 kilometres winds to the top from the small village of Porepunkah, but snow-chains must be carried at all times during the winter ski season. Apart from the chalet, there is also accommodation at the mountain's ski-resort.

Bright (Vic.) is the 'tourist capital' of the Ovens Valley, 300 kilometres north-east of Melbourne. The valley is the best place in Australia to see autumn colours, and in April–May each year Bright holds a festival to celebrate the beauty of the season. At this time thousands of visitors come to see the glorious abundance of colourful trees in the parks, gardens and streets, in the surrounding fields and along the banks of the streams. Bright is a town for all seasons: in winter it is the gateway to several ski-resorts; spring is heralded by rich displays of golden wattles in bloom, flowering fruit-trees and fresh greens of deciduous trees bursting into leaf; come summer, with its pleasant warm days and refreshingly cool nights, the town is an ideal spot for all kinds of summer activities, including walking on the nearby high plains to see the alpine wildflowers. This picture (*above*) shows Centenary Park in autumn.

37

Rivers and Lakes

The vital watershed for nearly half of the Australian continent is the Great Dividing Range in the east; without it, much of the country would be a useless wasteland. Its slopes give birth to a multitude of streams and rivers that carry their life-giving waters far out to the arid plains of the west; on the eastern side, after nourishing the fertile land between the ranges and the relatively small area to the coast, these rivers empty into the Pacific Ocean. The northern end of the Great Divide is in the tropics, so the many watercourses in that region are fed by heavy tropical rains that drench the ranges. The southern end lies in a cool temperate zone, where in winter the high ranges are blanketed in snow that abundantly feeds great rivers such as the Murray and the Snowy. A number of rivers are dammed, and many of the resulting manmade lakes are very beautiful.

Rivalling the dams in beauty are the diverse natural lakes. There are inland ponds fed by warm artesian springs, and coastal lakes separated from the ocean's strong surf only by a fragile barrier of sand-dunes. There are mountain tarns and glacial lakes in the southern high country; small and large lakes that fill old volcanic craters and dot the landscape from Queensland to South Australia; and in the wetlands of northern Australia, lagoons that brim with water after the annual monsoonal rains, only to recede over the dry season.

Because Western Australia has no high range to compare with the eastern watershed, this State has a much lower rainfall. Many of its rivers survive on barely adequate winter rains, and others may not flow properly for years. In the south-west, a number of relatively small ranges give rise to several streams, the most important being the Swan-Avon system which rises in the Darling Range.

In the outback, most of the lakes are dry saltpans; and the rivers are more commonly rivers of sand, flowing only after the occasional good rain. Rising in the few areas where ranges receive a low, erratic rainfall, the watercourses flow towards the deserts and salt lakes, but usually the insatiable sands soak up the liquid long before it reaches its destination. However, on the rare occasions when the lakes fill, they become great salty seas that can persist for months. Lake Eyre, which makes headlines whenever it fills, receives waters from a vast drainage system of more than a million square kilometres. But most of the time the salt lakes are thickly encrusted with glittering salt, a remarkable contrast to the blue and green softness of the mountain lakes of the east.

Kiewa River (Vic.) in autumn. This river rises by way of two main tributaries in the Bogong High Plains and Mount Hotham area, and flows through the beautiful Kiewa Valley to Lake Hume, on the Murray River. Part of the great Snowy Mountains Hydro-electric Scheme, its waters pass through the Kiewa hydro-electric stations situated on the headwaters, not far from the town of Mount Beauty. This very scenic river is a favourite with artists and photographers. The spot pictured (*above*) is near Tawonga, about 80 kilometres south of Wodonga, in Victoria's north-east.

Murray River at Mildura (Vic.). Australia's most important river, draining more than one-fifth of the continent in four States, the Murray rises in the Snowy Mountains and travels 2588 kilometres before entering the sea near Goolwa, in South Australia. Its waters irrigate thousands of farms, and provide a recreational ground for watersports and holiday houseboats. The loveliest sight on the river is the old paddle-steamers (*left*). In the nineteenth century they carried primary produce and supplies to and from towns and properties along the river; today they carry tourists wishing to relive a little history.

Mossman River Gorge (Qld) lies at the south-eastern corner of Daintree River National Park, four kilometres out of the town of Mossman, north of Cairns. Only a small part of the gorge is accessible, because it marks the start of a great wilderness region. From the carpark, a five-minute walking-track through the rainforest leads to several enchanting spots by the river, including a quiet pool suitable for swimming (the water is surprisingly cold); the river upstream from the pool is studded with boulders and whitewater rapids (*above*).

Saltpan, Simpson Desert. This desert spreads into parts of South Australia, Queensland and the Northern Territory. In South Australia, near the corner of the three States, there is a series of saltpans generally covered in gleaming white salt (*top right*). However, after good rains they brim with water — or hide a water-table just beneath the seemingly firm surface.

The Ord River (WA) is one of the great rivers of the east Kimberleys. After cyclonic rains its floodwaters are trapped in the Ord River Dam. This aerial view (*right*), with the Carr Boyd Range in the distance, is from near Kununurra.

The Snowy River rises on the slopes of Mount Kosciusko in the Snowy Mountains and empties into Bass Strait at Marlo in east Gippsland. For most of its 435-kilometre journey it flows through wild and rugged terrain, much of which is inaccessible except to whitewater canoeists. The view pictured (*above*) is in Kosciusko National Park, New South Wales, near the Victorian border. Near the border on both sides there are some lovely views of the Snowy as it runs by the Jindabyne–Buchan road; in a few spots it is possible to stop close to the river and walk along its banks.

The Ebor Falls (NSW) lie at the edge of the small New England town of Ebor, high in the Great Dividing Range 80 kilometres east of Armidale. Fed by the Guy Fawkes River, the falls form a series of cascades that are quite spectacular after heavy rains have fallen in the district. Lookouts have been erected in a number of places to give easy viewing of the falls; don't miss the lower falls, which can be seen only from the bottom carpark. Shown here (*right*) are the upper falls.

Dove Lake (Tas.) is part of the Cradle Mountain–Lake St Clair National Park, situated in the central highlands, 80 kilometres from Devonport. The lake's basin was gouged deeply by glacial actions during an earlier age, and has around its edge a number of small beaches covered with coarse white sand. From the Dove Lake carpark there are marvellous views of Cradle Mountain; in this scene (*above*) the mountain is reflected in the lake in a rare moment of stillness. The weather here is notoriously bad: if a day begins with promise, it is likely that after a few hours clouds will stream over the ranges, followed soon by heavy curtains of mist and rain which may obliterate everything for days. In summer, severe storms and even snow can sweep over the land. The park has many walking-paths, including the famous five-day Overland Track which links Cradle Mountain to Lake St Clair in the south. Because of the unpredictable weather, it is essential for all day-walkers to register their route with the ranger.

44

Near Glen Davis (NSW). This is a sunset view of a billabong that lies close to the Capertee River, which flows past the small settlement of Glen Davis in the Capertee Valley, 120 kilometres north of Lithgow. Bordered by high vertical sandstone cliffs that edge the Wollemi National Park to the east, the picturesque Capertee Valley is believed to be one of the largest enclosed valleys in the world. There are two entrances to it: from Capertee on the highway and from Rylstone near Mudgee. Glen Davis was a boom-town for a few years in the 1940s when shale-mining for synthetic oil was considered economically viable. By 1952, because of high production costs and the small quantities of shale available, the town closed—though people later started to return to live there. Today, Glen Davis serves local farmers, craftspeople, and an increasing number of tourists who come to see the beauty of the valley.

The Williams River (NSW), which runs through Barrington Tops National Park, 96 kilometres north-west of Newcastle, offers some splendid scenery from its banks (*above*). Barrington Tops is the plateau, 914 metres high, that forms a south-eastern spur from the Great Dividing Range. Often shrouded in mist, the old Antarctic-beech forest, snow-gum plains and subalpine woodlands give the Tops a special wilderness character. A dry-weather road goes only to the carpark, situated about halfway up; from there it is strictly four-wheel-drive country, or hard walking.

Lake St Clair (Tas.) lies at the southern end of the Cradle Mountain–Lake St Clair National Park. Access is easy: the lake is only five bitumen kilometres off the Lyell Highway, and visitors on their way to or from Queenstown can call in to Cynthia Bay (*top right*) where the camping ground, picnic area and rangers' station are located. Many excellent walks begin from here.

At Walker Flat (SA) pelicans are a common sight on the tranquil backwaters of the Murray River (*right*). Situated on a great bend of the Murray, about 100 kilometres east of Adelaide and just north of Mannum, Walker Flat is a popular spot for houseboats and other boating activities.

The Tropical North

Australia's tropical region covers the northern part of the country, and stretches from the Kimberley coast in the far north-west of Western Australia, across the top of the Northern Territory, to the far north of Queensland. Much of it encompasses vast tracts of wilderness. In the Kimberleys, grassy plains meet rugged and colourful ranges carved in many places by great rivers. In the Territory's Kakadu and Arnhem Land, and reaching across to Queensland's Gulf of Carpentaria and to Cape York Peninsula, there are wetlands made up of lily-studded lagoons, numerous watercourses, floodplains, and much wildlife; there are also areas of rough scrub and woodland, punctuated with giant anthills, stretching for hundreds of kilometres before giving way to networks of mangroves, swamps and mudflats patterned with meandering streams. In dramatic contrast to these regions are the rainforested hills and mountain-ranges of the far north's section of the Great Dividing Range, where a luxuriant world of dense vegetation contains a wealth of valuable flora and fauna. Large areas of tropical coast are still virgin ground, and in all probability will remain wilderness because of the difficulty of access either by land or by sea; other parts of the coast have become palm-fringed holiday resorts.

There are only two seasons in the north: the Wet and the Dry. During the wet season, which occurs between December and April, monsoonal and cyclonic rains deluge the country, transforming a parched, tired-looking land into one that is vibrantly green and pulsates with renewed vitality. The dry season falls between May and November, and, except on the slopes of the Great Divide, little or no rain falls during this time. The grey skies of the Wet change to blue, and the hot sun bakes the earth, shrinking lagoons and leaving strings of waterholes in the rivers. Unsealed roads are coated with dust instead of mud, and access to the popular tourist spots once again becomes easy.

Burning-off in the woodland takes place during the Dry, as it has for thousands of years: the vegetation needs the refining action of fire for its continuity, otherwise prolific growth would upset the ecological balance. The dry season is also the time when thousands of people migrate north in order to escape the cold southern winters. As the Dry ends, the humid weather becomes unbearably hot; by now most of the tourists have returned south. Eventually the stillness of the bush is shattered by violent storms and sheets of rain: the Wet has arrived, bringing much needed relief to the land and to all living creatures.

Katherine Gorge (NT) is one of the great tourist attractions of the north. Part of a large national park lying near the town of Katherine, some 300 kilometres south of Darwin, Katherine Gorge stretches for about 12 kilometres and consists of thirteen marvellous gorges that imprison the Katherine River. There are three ways to see the gorge: by boat, by plane, or by walking along the clifftops. Shown here (*above*) is the view from Pats lookout, on the Windolf clifftop walk. From here a track leads down the cliff to a large rocky ledge, which gives good access to the water for swimming.

Roper Creek (NT) is a tributary of the Roper River, a major coastal watercourse of the far north. The scene pictured (*left*) is at Mataranka, near the thermal springs: the cool air of a winter's morning causes the warm water in the creek to steam slightly. Mataranka's hot springs have become an important tourist attraction. Situated 450 kilometres south of Darwin, this beautiful thermal pool is a veritable oasis for weary travellers. The water temperature of 33°C may seem rather warm for swimming given that the air temperature is about the same, but it is surprisingly refreshing.

Cardwell (Qld) is situated beside the busy Bruce High
way, 58 kilometres north of Ingham. Much of the
foreshore (*above*) is lined with palms, bright flowering
bougainvillea and other tropical vegetation, and an early
morning walk along the narrow beach at high tide is a
delight; at low tide it is not so pleasant, as vast expanses
of mudflats are exposed and the sandflies come out with
a vengeance. Offshore lies Hinchinbrook Island, a large
and beautiful wilderness of mountains, superb beaches
and a maze of waterways and mangrove swamps. Day
trips to the island and the resort depart from Cardwell.

The Millaa Millaa Falls (Qld) are located on the Atherton
Tableland, behind Cairns. One of many in the area, this
beautiful waterfall lies in a picturesque clearing of lush
rainforest near the small town of Millaa Millaa; access is
via a narrow bitumen road which runs to the carpark
beside the falls. Although the main viewing area is just
below the carpark, a narrow path runs through the
rainforest on the left and takes you to the base of the
waterfall; this view (*right*) is from the path, near the
base.

At Innisfail (Qld), smoke from a sugarcane burnoff lightly veils the setting sun (*top left*). Lying by the Bruce Highway, 90 kilometres south of Cairns, Innisfail is the centre of a prosperous sugar-producing district. From June to about November the cane is burnt prior to cutting.

Lakefield National Park (Qld) covers an extensive area between Laura and Princess Charlotte Bay, on Cape York Peninsula. Featuring a network of watercourses, swamps, lagoons and an abundance of wildlife, this national park protects an important tropical wetland region. Pictured (*left*) is a lagoon near Laura.

The Barron River (Qld) rises near Herberton on the Atherton Tableland and empties its waters into Trinity Bay, just north of Cairns. It is shown here (*above*) as a young stream, at the top of Dinner Falls in Crater National Park, 21 kilometres from Herberton. From the carpark, a walking-track links an old volcanic crater with Dinner Falls, and passes through some superb rainforest. One of several national parks on the tableland, Crater National Park is a good place to see—and hear—the spotted catbird, whose call sounds remarkably like that of a wailing cat.

Kakadu (NT), created a national park in 1979, lies about 250 kilometres east of Darwin at the edge of Arnhem Land. It is one of the most important national parks in Australia; but because there are some uranium mines situated in and around it, the park faces potential problems. It is being well looked after by the rangers, a fact obvious to anyone who was familiar with the area before it was declared a national park. Kakadu covers a vast area, comprising tropical woodlands, weathered rocky outliers, sandstone escarpments and wetlands (*above*); the park also preserves a rich heritage of Aboriginal culture.

The saltwater crocodile (*right*) lives in estuaries, rivers and lagoons of far-northern Australia, including Kakadu National Park. Popularly called the 'salty', and very territorial in behaviour, this extremely dangerous reptile has taken a number of lives in recent years; tourists should heed the notices that warn against swimming which are now placed beside many rivers and lagoons (but by no means all) throughout the north. Since 1971 this crocodile has been protected by law, because hunters had reduced its numbers to very low levels. The one pictured is 'Charlie', at Hartley Creek Zoo, near Cairns.

Yellow Water Lagoon, in Kakadu National Park (NT), is a magical sight at moonset (*above*). This large lagoon is fed by the Jim Jim Creek.

Nourlangie Rock (*overleaf*), also in Kakadu National Park, rises to 265 metres to form an outlier of the west escarpment of Arnhem Land.

Galvans Gorge (WA) is in the Phillips Range, 360
kilometres north-east of Derby in the west Kimberleys.
Access is easy, as the gorge lies only one kilometre off
the Gibb River beef road just south of Mount Barnett
Station (the only place that sells petrol along this 710-
kilometre road). From the carpark it is a good five
minutes' walk to the gorge's beautiful pool (*above*), the
surrounding lush vegetation and the waterfall, which in
the dry season is only a small trickle. This gorge is one of
a number lying off the Gibb River road. Compared with
other places in Australia, tourism in the Kimberleys is
relatively new; indeed, Galvans Gorge was not even
named until the early 1970s, when the West Kimberley
Shire Council decided to honour Ivars Janis ('Joe') Galvans
for his assistance in developing local tourism by leading
a party of about twelve vehicles to the gorge in 1971.

Boab trees at sunset. Boab—or baobab—trees are a distinct feature of the Kimberley region. Growing only in the north-west corner of Western Australia, the boab (*Adansonia gregorii*) is one of only two species, the other originating in Africa. Capable of reaching many centuries in age, the old ones have girths out of all proportion to their heights: some attain a circumference of up to 24 metres. The trunks act as storage reservoirs for food and moisture. These trees have leaves only during the wet season, and for the rest of the year their bare, untidy limbs resemble roots more than branches. The nut-like fruit has a dry pulp which tastes like cream of tartar and is said to be refreshing in humid weather; and the nuts are collected by the Aborigines, who carve exquisite designs on them. A popular name for the boab is 'bottle-tree', though it is not to be confused with the bottle-shaped trees of Queensland that belong to the genus *Brachychiton*.

The Outback

The term 'outback' applies to the land lying well beyond the coastal cities and towns, the settled areas, and the green slopes of the Great Dividing Range: this means that it covers more than three-quarters of the continent. The Australian outback is a place of endless plains, stony and red-sand deserts, strange monoliths, and rugged rocky ranges slashed with incredible gorges. It is harsh and inhospitable, sparsely populated, and should not be taken lightly by travellers, however experienced. But despite the severity of the region, there is little doubt that this vast area contains some of the most unusual and thrilling scenery in Australia—indeed, in the world.

Colour dominates much of the outback. No scene is the same in the morning as in the afternoon, at sunrise as at sunset, for the land responds wonderfully to the changes of light as the sun progresses across the sky. In the first and last rays of the sun, sand-dunes change into hills of blood-red splendour and distant ranges become poems of pinks and mauves. Rocks, gorges and the great monoliths such as Ayers Rock, the Olgas, Mount Conner and Chambers Pillar undergo superb colour-changes in the course of a day, involving purples, pinks, reds, rusts and browns. If clouds are present at sunrise or sunset, the colours are even more intense.

A good portion of the outback pushes into the tropical regions of northern Australia; the climate in this part is more stable, with its two distinct seasons, the Wet and the Dry. In the central areas of the continent the climate can be unpredictable, since normal weather-patterns are frequently disrupted by droughts or excessive rains. An area that has an accepted annual rainfall of around 125 millimetres may see years pass without a shower of rain; instead, storms of dust choke the land. Then a number of good seasons might follow in which the average annual rainfall is trebled, causing the normally dry rivers and creeks to come down in flood, and the roads to turn into quagmires of mud that are often impassable for days. When the rain does come, the land is miraculously transformed: wildflowers bloom, and plants not seen for years may appear. Even the wildlife becomes more abundant. As the sun warms shallow waterholes, several species of primitive shrimp hatch from eggs that have remained unharmed by drought, sometimes waiting decades for the right conditions.

Regardless of the vagaries of the seasons, the summers are always very hot, and the winters pleasant but with extremely cold nights. The best time to travel through the outback is between April and October.

Near Kununurra (WA). This is a typical scene of the far
north-west outback in the Kimberley region, during the
dry season: a sea of golden cane-grass, graced by a few
boabs and evergreen trees, sweeps towards a distant
warm-coloured craggy range (*above*). The town of
Kununurra is situated in the east Kimberleys, 43 kilometres from the Northern Territory border. Built in
1960, it is the centre for the Ord River irrigation and
agriculture scheme, and for an increasingly busy tourist
industry; it is also the closest town to the Argyle diamond
mine, south of Lake Argyle.

Trephina Gorge (NT) is situated 76 kilometres from
Alice Springs in the eastern MacDonnell Ranges, near
the Ross River tourist resort. This gorge is renowned for
its splendid walls of craggy red rock which rise pre-
cipitously from the floor of Trephina Creek. At sunrise
the great bastions of rock at the entrance to the gorge
flare a rich crimson-orange (*left*). The road into Trephina
crosses the sandy creekbed, but unless the river is
flowing it is generally passable to all types of vehicles.

The Devils Marbles (NT) would be Australia's most
popular collection of rocks, and most travellers on their
way north, or south, stop to wander among them.
Situated 100 kilometres south of Tennant Creek, in the
Devils Marbles Reserve, these fascinating boulders lie
scattered for many hectares beside the busy Stuart
Highway, which links Alice Springs with Darwin. The
Marbles appear in many shapes and sizes: some stand
alone, while others, resembling great buns, are piled on
top of each other. All show some degree of roundness, or
of softening at the edges. They were formed over time by
sharp changes in temperature, and by weathering that
caused erosion along the joints of the original granite
mass; the rocks were then rounded to their present
shapes by the elements. Growing close to some of the
boulders are ghost gums, their slender shapes dwarfed
by the monstrous tors.

Ormiston Gorge (NT) is the most impressive of all the numerous gorges that slash the colourful MacDonnell Ranges in central Australia. Part of the largest national park in the western MacDonnells, Ormiston Gorge lies off the Glen Helen road, 134 kilometres from Alice Springs. Access is possible for all types of vehicles, as a bitumen road leads to the carpark by the camping ground. The craggy, many-hued walls of the gorge rise to 200 metres as they follow the twisting stony bed of Ormiston Creek. The large waterhole at the gorge's entrance is permanent, even during drought, and on still mornings the reflections of the ghost and river gums, of the rocky cliffs and of the fallen boulders are breathtakingly beautiful. To appreciate the size of this magnificent gorge, it is necessary for the visitor to walk right through to Ormiston Pound, a moderately flat area lying beyond the gorge and the enclosing mountains, of which the most dominant is Mount Giles.

Sturt's Stony Desert (*above*) lies chiefly between Cooper Creek and the Diamantina River in north-eastern South Australia and south-western Queensland. It is probably the grimmest of Australia's six major deserts. Despite the hard stones, after rain the ground is treacherously soft for vehicles.

Escott Station (*left*) is a large cattle property near Burketown in Queensland, close to the Gulf of Carpentaria.

Erldunda (*above*) lies in the red sandhill country of central Australia, where some of the loveliest stands of desert oaks are seen. In spring many of the dunes are garlanded with wildflowers.

Mirra Mitta Bore (*right*) is one of many hot artesian bores situated along the Birdsville Track, which runs from Marree in South Australia to Birdsville in Queensland.

Palm Valley (NT) is situated on a tributary of the Finke River and shelters a small pocket of ancient cycads and Livistona palms, remnants of the time when central Australia was covered with tropical vegetation. Some of the loveliest sights here are to be seen at the still pools of water that mirror the ancient palms (*above*). Part of the Finke Gorge National Park, which includes the grand Krichauff Range and the Amphitheatre, Palm Valley lies about 140 kilometres south-west of Alice Springs. The last 16 kilometres into the valley are strictly for four-wheel-drive vehicles because the track follows the deep sandy bed of the Finke River.

Weano Gorge (WA) is one of the deep chocolate-coloured gorges that fissure the iron-ore-rich plateau of the Hamersley Range, the State's highest landmass, which stretches for nearly 400 kilometres across the Pilbara in the north-west. Part of the range is a national park, lying near Wittenoom, 300 kilometres from Port Hedland on the coast. Although it is possible to climb down into a few of the gorges—Weano being one of them—most people prefer to view them from the top; some of the gorges are very narrow and have terrifyingly sheer walls, dropping to 150 metres in places. This view (*right*) is from deep within Weano Gorge.

Great Tourist Attractions

Most countries have particular places and features of distinction that are considered 'musts' for visitors to see. Heading the list in Australia are the Great Barrier Reef and Ayers Rock, two of the world's outstanding natural wonders. The Barrier Reef is the largest structure created by any living thing (including humans); it is also the greatest coral reef in the world, giving shelter to an enormous variety of marine life. Colourful Ayers Rock is the biggest single piece of exposed rock on the earth's surface, and lies in Uluru National Park in central Australia. Equally spectacular, and in a way more interesting, are the Olgas, not far from the Rock. They form an extraordinary circle of domes, red and bare, that from a distance appear to be piled high upon each other.

Many of the country's animals are attractions. A highlight for visitors to Melbourne is a trip to Phillip Island to see the Penguin Parade: every evening at dusk spectators watch from behind rails as hundreds of engaging fairy penguins come in from the sea and waddle up the floodlit beach to their burrows in the dunes. Zoos such as the Healesville Sanctuary close to Melbourne, Lone Pine Sanctuary in Brisbane, and Sydney's Taronga Zoo are excellent places to view a wide variety of Australian fauna. In Western Australia the wildflowers attract thousands of visitors every spring.

Of the historical attractions, probably the old penal-colony ruins at Port Arthur in Tasmania, and the reconstructed goldmining town of Sovereign Hill at Ballarat in Victoria, are the most famous. Then there are the priceless Aboriginal rock-art galleries of northern Australia, some of the most significant being the ones in Kakadu National Park.

Although the whole of central Australia, with its colourful ranges, unusual gorges and white-barked ghost gums, is an enormous drawcard, one of its most popular destinations is the opal-mining town of Coober Pedy in South Australia. In this unique town, most of the population lives underground in order to escape the dust and heat (summer temperatures can stay above 40°C for days on end), and even the churches, and some motels, museums and shops, are underground. Central Australia also features one of the country's most unusual events: Henley-on-Todd, a regatta in Alice Springs held annually in the sandy bed of the Todd River, with the 'boats' powered only by human legs. The finale is the great 'sea-battle', and one suspects that this rather wild but crowd-pleasing event could occur only in the Territory.

Ayers Rock (NT), in Uluru National Park, is situated 450 kilometres south-west of Alice Springs. Considered one of the great natural wonders of the world, this colossal red sandstone monolith has a circumference of nearly 9·5 kilometres and rises to 348 metres above the surrounding plain. The Rock's surface is fissured with deep gullies, ridges, and a multitude of rockholes that brim with water after rain, sending waterfalls cascading over the sheer walls. For the Aborigines the Rock is a ritual ground of sacred Dreamtime legends; for other people it is a unique tourist attraction.

The Olgas (NT), in Uluru National Park, lie 32 kilometres west of Ayers Rock. These wonderful sandstone domes were fashioned by the elements over the ages, and like Ayers Rock they undergo some incredible colour-changes. The view shown here (*above*) is at sunrise, from the lookout at the top of Katajuta, the only dome that is easy to climb. The highest is Mount Olga, rising 546 metres from the sandy plain. The domes are separated by ravines that support a surprising abundance of plantlife, sustained by moisture trapped in the sheltered gullies. There is some good walking in these lovely ravines, the well-known ones being Mount Olga Gorge, the Valley of the Winds, and the Valley of the Mice Women.

The Great Barrier Reef extends for 2000 kilometres along the east coast of Queensland, from the Torres Strait in the north to Gladstone in the south. There are many points of access from the mainland and island resorts, and one of the best is from Port Douglas, north of Cairns: daily, big catamarans travel to the Agincourt Reef, rated as one of the most spectacular on the outer barrier, and moor beside permanently based pontoons. The one shown here (*right*) is the Quicksilver pontoon. From it, visitors can view the coral in an underwater observatory, or take a trip in one of the semi-submersible boats in which the actual viewing room is a couple of metres below the water; they can also go snorkelling or scuba-diving. Marine biologists from Reef Biosearch give talks about the reef, and take interested people on guided snorkelling and diving tours through the coral wonderland that surrounds the pontoon. Another excellent day trip from Port Douglas is to Low Isle (*above*), a coral cay fringed with a sandy beach and tropical vegetation. From a pontoon, glass-bottomed boats take visitors to view the coral, and on to see the cay. The third picture (*top right*) shows a typical underwater coral scene.

The 'sea-battle', Henley-on-Todd (*top left*), is the last event of this fun regatta held annually at Alice Springs (NT). The battle is at its height: the 'ships' are powerful four-wheel-drive vehicles suitably dressed as floats (and armed) for the occasion, manned by crews of tough Territorians. The winner is the 'ship' last bogged in the sand—or the last to run out of ammunition.

Rock paintings, Kakadu (NT). Throughout this national park there are many superb galleries of Aboriginal paintings, recognized to be the finest of their type in the world. They are found in the overhanging shelters of rocky outliers, and present a vital record of human occupation of the area. The ones shown (*left*) are at Nourlangie Rock.

Port Arthur (Tas.), a notorious penitentiary in the years between 1830 and 1877, is now an important historic site and tourist attraction. It lies on the Tasman Peninsula in a national park, beyond the narrow isthmus at Eagle-hawk Neck. The isthmus presented a natural barrier that was relatively easy to guard, especially when fierce dogs were tethered across its 71 metres. Pictured (*above*) is the burnt-out shell of the convict-built church, one of Australia's most picturesque ruins.

Coober Pedy (SA) has been called the opal capital of the world. Situated on the Stuart Highway about halfway between Alice Springs and Port Augusta, this extraordinary opal-mining town has more than 70 opal fields, and sixteen opal shops that sell the precious stone to tourists. Apart from the buying of opals, there are plenty of attractions at Coober Pedy, many of them underground. The Old Timer's Mine (*above*)—a museum within a mine, complete with pockets of opals in the walls—gives visitors an excellent idea of mining conditions in the early years.

Wildflowers (WA). Western Australia is known as the Wildflower State: half of the continent's total number of species are found here. This carpet of everlasting daisies (*top right*) is near Mount Magnet, 350 kilometres east of Geraldton on the coast. The best month to see wildflowers in this inland area is September, provided adequate winter rains have fallen.

The Penguin Parade, Phillip Island (Vic.), takes place every evening at Summerland Beach, near the southwestern tip of the island, 120 kilometres from Melbourne. In this picture (*right*) the birds are approaching their burrows. The fairy penguin is the world's smallest penguin, and those on Phillip Island belong to one of the largest and most accessible colonies on Australia's southern seaboard.

Fauna and Flora

Australia's extraordinary diversity of fauna and flora is as fascinating as its scenery. Ranging widely in form an colour, most of the species are unique, and many of the animals have no 'relatives' in other parts of the world: it little wonder that the early explorers and zoologists were amazed to come upon such creatures as kangaroo koalas, wombats, echidnas and platypuses. Australia is the world's stronghold of marsupials—pouched anima whose offspring are born at an undeveloped stage, leaving the mother's womb to crawl to her pouch where the mil is supplied. These animals colonized Australia before it was cut off from a greater landmass during the period continental separation and drift, and this allowed them time to develop in a region relatively free from predators.

There are more than 700 species of birds in Australia. Many of them are richly coloured, particularly the parrot while others are famous for their peculiar if somewhat raucous calls: for example, the kookaburras and cockatoo There are those with astonishing habits, such as the dancing lyrebirds and the decorating bowerbirds. Some of th larger birds are quite spectacular, among them the emu, the cassowary and the brolga.

Australia is a paradise for herpetologists. There are around 110 species of snakes, and more than 300 lizards the largest of the latter being the great perentie, a goanna that can grow to 2·5 metres in length. Two crocodile inhabit areas of the north: the harmless freshwater crocodile and the dangerous estuarine one. In addition, there a more than 100 species of frog, nine kinds of freshwater tortoise, and four varieties of turtle.

The country's plants are just as intriguing as the wildlife. With approximately 15 000 species of flora growing a wide range of habitats, Australia has more plants endemic to its area than any other country—and new kinds a discovered every year. Many come in strange forms: for example, the banksias, the bottlebrushes and the kangaro paws. By far the richest wildflower areas lie in the sandplains of Western Australia. Many plant species are nativ to that State: of the 58 species of banksia, for instance, 45 are confined to the west. In the east, Victoria Grampians harbour about one-third of the State's indigenous flora; Queensland's Lamington Plateau near Brisban is well known for its orchids; and South Australia's best wildflower region is the Flinders Ranges.

The frilled lizard (*above*) is found throughout woodland areas of northern Australia, and can grow to 90 centimetres in length. When danger threatens, this lizard will face its opponent and erect its spectacular neck frill. The Queensland specimens are a grey colour, but those found in the Northern Territory and Western Australia display frills tinted with warm reds and oranges.

An eastern grey kangaroo (*left*), with a baby joey in her pouch. Ranging throughout eastern Australia, this kangaroo is one of about 50 species of macropods, a family that includes the wallabies, the rat-kangaroos and the tree-kangaroos.

The laughing kookaburra (*right*), named for its ringing, cheerful laugh, is one of Australia's best-loved birds. Belonging to the kingfisher family, it is native to eastern Australia but was introduced to Tasmania and the west in the early 1900s. It lives in woodlands and open forests—and in urban areas if there are plenty of trees.

The echidna, or spiny anteater (*above*), widely distributed throughout Australia, is an egg-laying mammal and has a diet consisting mainly of ants. When frightened or attacked, it rolls into a pincushion-like ball and clings to the ground with its strong claws.

The dingo, or warrigal (*top left*), is believed to have evolved from a domesticated version of the Asiatic wolf which accompanied the first Aborigines to the continent and afterwards to have turned wild. Unable to bark, it is known for its eerie, long-drawn-out howls, and inhabits inland Australia.

Koalas (*right*), among the most endearing of all the marsupials, are confined largely to Victoria, the coastal forests of New South Wales and parts of Queensland. These nocturnal animals feed mainly at night, selecting leaves from only about twelve of the 500-odd species of eucalypts; seldom do they drink. The adult male utters the most extraordinary call, which sounds remarkably like the exhaust of a motorbike. The koalas pictured here are in the Lone Pine Sanctuary, Brisbane.

Southern mahogany, *Eucalyptus botryoides* (*above*), found only on the east coast, from Newcastle south to east Gippsland.

Sturt's desert pea, *Clianthus formosus* (*top left*), grows throughout the Australian inland after good rains.

Hooker's banksia, *Banksia hookerana* (*left*), is confined to a small area south of Geraldton, Western Australia.

Fairies' aprons, *Utricularia dichotoma* (*below*), favour swampy areas of the eastern States.